The New
Common
Denominator
of
SUCCESS

ALBERT E. N. GRAY

TREMENDOUS
LIFE BOOKS

Life-Changing Classics, Volume XIX

The New Common Denominator of Success

Published by
Tremendous Life Books
206 West Allen Street
Mechanicsburg, PA 17055
717-766-9499   800-233-2665
Fax: 717-766-6565
www.TremendousLifeBooks.com

ISBN: 978-1-933715-73-5

Cover Design and Interior Layout
by Gregory Dixon

Printed in the United States of America

Table of Contents

Success is reached by being active, awake, ahead of the crowd, by aiming high, pushing ahead, honestly, diligently, patiently; by climbing, digging, saving; by forgetting the past, using the present, trusting in the future; by honoring God, having a purpose, fainting not, determining to win, and striving to the end.

Russell Conwell

Foreword by Charlie "T" Jones

If there were a Hall of Fame for motivational books, *The Common Denominator of Success* would be listed in the top ten. I began my selling career at age 6 in 1933 and never stopped selling. At age 22 I became a life insurance salesman and fortunately for me, my manager gave me a little booklet with the most wisdom in the fewest words I had ever read. Now fifty eight years later, it is still the most wisdom in the fewest words I've ever read. The simple truth of this book did more than impact my life, it became my calling card. I noticed many discarded my business card, and some while I was still in their office. Having the gift of common sense, I decided I would discontinue business cards and give them *The Common Denominator of Success* with my name and phone number stamped inside the cover. They always were surprised with my unique approach and expressed their appreciation. When they read it they never forgot me and many times asked me where they could get some for their employees or customers. Over the years, I've skimmed and read thousands of books but none have impacted my thinking and actions more than this one.

In *The New Common Denominator of Success* I haven't changed a word of its tremendous message but I have revised it for every profession, young or old, male or female.

I'm humbled and honored to write the foreword to this little classic that has helped me enjoy a life of doing what I don't like to do. Today this may be the only book that emphasizes the point that only your purpose can enable you to do the things that you don't like to do, in order to enjoy a truly, tremendously fulfilled life.

Tremendously,
Charles "T" Jones
Author of *Life is Tremendous*

The New
Common Denominator
of Success

Several years ago I was brought face to face with the very disturbing realization that I was trying to supervise and direct the efforts of a large number of men who were trying to achieve success, without knowing myself what the secret of success really was. And that, naturally, brought me face to face with the further realization that regardless of what other knowledge I might have brought to my job, I was definitely lacking in the most important knowledge of all.

Of course, like most of us, I had been brought up on the popular belief that the secret of success is hard work, but I had seen so many men work hard without

What our deepest self craves is not mere enjoyment, but some supreme purpose that will enlist all our powers and will give unity and direction to our life. We can never know the profoundest joy without a conviction that our life is significant—not a meaningless episode. The loftiest aim of human life is the ethical perfecting of mankind—the transfiguration of humanity.

Henry J. Golding

succeeding and so many men succeed without working hard that I had become convinced that hard work was not the real secret even though in most cases it might be one of the requirements.

And so I set out on a voyage of discovery which carried me through biographies and autobiographies and all sorts of dissertations on success and the lives of successful men until I finally reached a point at which I realized that the secret I was trying to discover lay not only in what men did, but also in what made them do it.

I realized further that the secret for which I was searching must not only apply to every definition of success, but since it must apply to everyone to whom it was offered, it must also apply to everyone who had ever been successful. In short, I was looking for the common denominator of success.

And because that is exactly what I was looking for, that is exactly what I found.

The goal of life is imminent in each moment, each thought, word, act, and does not have to be sought apart from these. It consists in no specific achievement, but the state of mind in which everything is done, the quality infused into existence. The function of man is not to attain an object, but to fulfill a purpose; not to accomplish but to be accomplished.

S.E. Stanton

But this common denominator of success is so big, so powerful, and so vitally important to your future and mine that I'm not going to make a speech about it. I'm just going to "lay it on the line" in words of one syllable, so simple that everyone can understand them.

The common denominator of success— the secret of success of every person who has ever been successful—lies in the fact that he or she formed the habit of doing things that failures don't like to do.

It's just as true as it sounds and it's just as simple as it seems. You can hold it up to the light, you can put it to the acid test, and you can kick it around until it's worn out, but when you are all through with it, it will still be the common denominator of success, whether you like it or not.

It will still explain why many come into business with every apparent qualification for success and give us the most disappointing failures, while others come in and

All the world over it is true that a double-minded man is unstable in all his ways, like a wave on the stream-let, tossed hither and thither with every eddy of its tide. A determined purpose in life and a steady adhiesion to it through all disadvantages, are indispensable conditions of success.

William M. Punshon

Great minds have great pur-poses, others have wishes. Little minds are tamed and subdued by misfortune; but great minds rise above them.

Washington Irving

achieve outstanding success in spite of many obvious and discouraging handicaps. And since it will also explain your future, it would seem to be a mighty good idea for you to use it in determining just what sort of a future you are going to have. In other words, let's take this big, all-embracing secret and boil it down to fit the individual you.

If the secret of success lies in forming the habit of doing things that failures don't like to do, let's start the boiling-down process by determining what are the things that failures don't like to do. The things that failures don't like to do are the very things that you and I and other human beings, including successful men, naturally don't like to do. In other words, we've got to realize right from the start that success is something which is achieved by the minority, and is therefore unnatural and not to be achieved by following our natural likes and dislikes nor by being guided by our natural preferences and prejudices.

There is one quality more important than know-how, and we cannot accuse the U.S. of any undue amount of it. This is know-how by which we determine not only how to accomplish our purposes, but what our purposes are to be.

Norbert Wiener

The only true happiness comes from squandering ourselves for a purpose.

John Mason Brown

The things that failures don't like to do, in general, are too obvious for us to discuss them here, and so, since our success is to be achieved in sales, let us move on to a discussion of the things that we don't like to do. Here, too, the things we don't like to do are too many to permit specific discussion, but I think they can all be disposed of by saying that they all emanate from one basic dislike peculiar to our type of selling. We don't like to call on people who don't want to see us and talk to them about something they don't want to talk about. Any reluctance to follow a definite prospecting program, to use prepared sales talks, to organize time and to organize effort are all caused by this one basic dislike.

Perhaps you have wondered what is behind this peculiar lack of welcome on the part of our prospective buyers. Isn't it due to the fact that our prospects are human too? And isn't it true that the average human being is not big enough to buy of his own accord and is therefore prone

I have brought myself by long meditation to the conviction that a human being with a settled purpose must accomplish it, and that nothing can resist a will which will stake even existence upon its fulfillment.

Benjamin Disraeli

My business is not to remake myself, but to make the absolute best of what God made.

Robert Browning

to escape our efforts to make him bigger or persuade him to do something he doesn't want to do by striking at the most important weakness we possess: namely, our desire to be appreciated? Perhaps you have been discouraged by a feeling that you were born subject to certain dislikes peculiar to you, with which the successful in our business are not afflicted.

Perhaps you have wondered why it is that the biggest producers seem to like to do the things that you don't like to do.

They don't! And I think this is the most encouraging statement I have ever offered to a group of professionals.

But if they don't like to do these things, then why do they do them? Because by doing the things they don't like to do, they can accomplish the things they want to accomplish. The successful are influenced by the desire for pleasing results. Failures are influenced by the desire for pleasing methods and are inclined to be

A great river is not aimless. It has direction and purpose. So also must a good life have a definite aim; all its strength and fullness must be turned in one direction. To many the whole object of life is work. Ask a man what he is doing with his life and ninety-nine times out of a hundred he will reply by telling you his trade or profession.

Grenville Kleiser

satisfied with such results as can be obtained by doing things they like to do.

Why are the successful able to do things they don't like to do while failures are not? Because the successful have a **purpose** strong enough to make them form the habit of doing things they don't like to do in order to accomplish the **purpose** they want to accomplish.

Sometimes even our best producers get into a slump. When a person goes into a slump, it simply means that he has reached a point at which, for the time being, the things he doesn't like to do have become more important than his reasons for doing them. And may I pause to suggest to you managers that when one of your good producers goes into a slump, the less you talk about his production and the more you talk about his **purpose**, the sooner you will pull him out of his slump?

Many with whom I have discussed this

Thy purpose firm is equal to
the deed. Who does the best
his circumstances allows,
does well, acts nobly;
angels could no more.

Young

The purpose of life is a life
of purpose.

Robert Byrne

common denominator of success have said at this point, "But I have a family to support and I have to have a living for my family and myself. Isn't that enough of a **purpose**?"

No, it isn't. It isn't a sufficiently strong **purpose** to make you form the habit of doing the things you don't like to do for the very simple reasons that it is easier to adjust ourselves to the hardships of a poor living than it is to adjust ourselves to the hardships of making a better one. If you doubt me, just think of all the things you are willing to go without in order to avoid doing the things you don't like to do. All of which seems to prove that the strength which holds you to your **purpose** is not your own strength but the strength of the **purpose** itself.

Now let's see why habit belongs so importantly in this common denominator of success.

We are creatures of habit just as machines

It is better by a noble bold-
ness to run the risk of being
subject to half of the evils
we anticipate, than to
remain in cowardly listless-
ness for fear of what may
happen.

Herodotus

Above all, be of single aim;
have a legitimate and useful
purpose, and devote your-
self unreservedly to it.

James Lane Allen

are creatures of momentum, for habit is nothing more or less than momentum translated from the concrete into the abstract. Can you picture the problem that would face our mechanical engineers if there were no such thing as momentum? Speed would be impossible because the highest speed at which any vehicle could be moved would be the first speed at which it could be broken away from a standstill. Elevators could not be made to rise, airplanes could not be made to fly, and the entire world of mechanics would find itself in a total state of helplessness. Then who are you and I to think that we can do with our own human nature what the finest engineers in the world could not do with the finest machinery that was ever built?

Every single qualification for success is acquired through habit. We form habits and habits form futures. If you do not deliberately form good habits, then unconsciously you will form bad ones. You are the kind of person you are because you have formed the habit of being that kind

What men want is not talent, it is purpose; in other words, not the power to achieve, but will to labor. I believe that labor judiciously and continuously applied becomes genius.

Edward Bulwer-Lytton

More men fail through lack of purpose than lack of talent.

Billy Sunday

Have a purpose for everything you do. Study, work, travel, etc. Live for a purpose.

A.A.M.

of person, and the only way you can change is through habit.

The success habits in selling are divided into four main groups:

Prospecting habits
Calling habits
Selling habits
Working habits

Let's discuss these habit groups in their order.

Any successful salesman will tell you that it is easier to sell to people who don't want it than it is to find people who do want it, but if you have not deliberately formed the habit of prospecting for needs, regardless of wants, then unconsciously you have formed the habit of limiting your prospecting to people who want your product or service and therein lies the one and only real reason for lack of prospects.

As to calling habits, unless you have

He who wishes to fulfill his mission in the world must be a man of one idea, that is, of one great overmastering purpose, overshadowing all his aims, and guiding and controlling his entire life.

Julius Bate

I determined never to stop until I had come to the end and achieved my purpose.

David Livingstone

deliberately formed the habit of calling on people who are able to buy but unwilling to listen, then unconsciously you have formed the habit of calling on people who are willing to listen but unable to buy.

As to selling habits, unless you have deliberately formed the habit of calling on prospects determined to make them see their reasons for buying your product, then unconsciously you have formed the habit of calling on prospects in a state of mind in which you are willing to let them make you see their reasons for not buying it.

As to working habits, if you will take care of the other three groups, the working habits will generally take care of themselves because under working habits are included study and preparation, organization of time and efforts, records, analyses, etc. Certainly you're not going to take the trouble to learn interest-arousing approaches and sales talks unless you're going to use them. You're not going to

A man's life may stagnate
as literally as water may
stagnate, and just as motion
and direction are the remedy for one, so purpose and
activity are the remedy for
the other.

John Burroughs

The purpose of human life
is to serve, and to show
compassion and the will to
help others.

Albert Schweitzer

plan your day's work when you know in your heart that you're not going to carry out your plans. And you're certainly not going to keep an honest record of things you haven't done or of results you haven't achieved. So let's not worry so much about the fourth group of success habits, for if you are taking care of the first three groups, most of the working habits will take care of themselves and you'll be able to afford a secretary to take care of the rest of them for you.

But before you decide to adopt these success habits, let me warn you of the importance of habit to your decision. I have attended many sales meetings and sales congresses during the past ten years and have often wondered why, in spite of the fact that there is so much good in them, so many seem to get so little lasting good out of them. Perhaps you have attended sales meetings in the past and have left determined to do the things that would make you successful or more successful only to find your decision or determination

Have a purpose in life, and having it, throw into your work such strength of mind and muscle as God has given you.

Thomas Carlyle

You can have anything you want—if you want it badly enough. You can be anything you want to be, do anything you set out to accomplish if you hold to that desire with singleness of purpose.

Abraham Lincoln

waning at just the time when it should be put into effect or practice.

Here's the answer. Any resolution or decision you make is simply a promise to yourself, which isn't worth a thing unless you have formed the habit of making it and keeping it. And you won't form the habit of making it and keeping it unless right at the start you link it with a definite **purpose** that can be accomplished by keeping it. In other words, any resolution or decision you make today has to be made again tomorrow, and the next day, and the next, and the next, and so on. And it not only has to be made each day, but it has to be kept each day, for if you miss one day in the making or keeping of it, you've got to go back and begin all over again. But if you continue the process of making it each morning and keeping it each day, you will finally wake up some morning a different person in a different world, and you will wonder what has happened to you and the world you used to live in.

Nothing contributes so much to tranquilizing the mind as a steady purpose— a point on which the soul may fix its intellectual eye.

Mary Wollstonecraft Shelley

There is no road to success but through a clear strong purpose. Nothing can take its place. A purpose underlies character, culture, position, attainment of every sort.

Theodore T. Munger

Here's what has happened. Your resolution or decision has become a habit and you don't have to make it on this particular morning. And the reason for your seeming like a different person living in a different world lies in the fact that for the first time in your life, you have become master of yourself and master of your likes and dislikes by surrendering to your **purpose** in life. That is why behind every success there must be a **purpose** and that is what makes **purpose** so important to your future. For in the last analysis, your future is not going to depend on economic conditions or outside influences of circumstances over which you have no control. Your future is going to depend on your **purpose** in life. So let's talk about **purpose**.

First of all, your **purpose** must be practical and not visionary. Some time ago, I talked with a person who thought he had a **purpose** which was more important to him than income. He was interested in the sufferings of his fellow man, and he want-

Find a purpose in life so big it will challenge every capacity to be at your best.

David O. Mckay

It is the old lesson—a worthy purpose, patient energy for its accomplishment, a resoluteness undaunted by difficulties, and then success.

W.M. Punshon

The purpose of life is not to be happy. It is to be useful, to be honorable, to be compassionate, to have it make some difference that you have lived and lived well.

Ralph Waldo Emerson

ed to be placed in a position to alleviate that suffering. But when he analyzed his real feeling, we discovered, and he admitted it, that what he really wanted was a real nice job dispensing charity with other people's money and being well paid for it, along with the appreciation and feeling of importance that would naturally go with such a job.

But in making your **purpose** practical, be careful not to make it logical. Make it a **purpose** of the sentimental or emotional type. Remember needs are logical while wants and desires are sentimental and emotional. Your needs will push you just so far, but when your needs are satisfied, they will stop pushing you. If, however, your **purpose** is in terms of wants and desires, then your wants and desires will keep pushing you long after your needs are satisfied and until your wants and desires are fulfilled.

Recently I was talking with a young man who long ago discovered the common

That man who forms a purpose which he knows to be right, and then moves forward to accomplish it without inquiring where it will land him as an individual, and without caring what the immediate consequences to himself will be, is the manliest of manly men.

John Wanamaker

denominator of success without identifying his discovery. He had a definite **purpose** in life and it was definitely a sentimental or emotional **purpose**. He wanted his boy to go through college without having to work his way through as he had done. He wanted to avoid for his little girl the hardships which his own sister had to face in her childhood. And he wanted his wife and the mother of his children to enjoy the luxuries and comforts, and even necessities, which had been denied his own mother. And he was willing to form the habit of doing things he didn't like to do in order to accomplish this **purpose**.

Not to discourage him, but rather to have him encourage me, I said to him, "Aren't you going a little too far with this thing? There's no logical reason why your son shouldn't be willing and able to work his way through college just as his father did. Of course he'll miss many of the things that you missed in your college life and he'll probably have heartaches and disappoint-

Thoughts lead on to purposes; purposes go forth in action; actions form habits; habits decide character; and character fixes our destiny.

Tryon Edwards

The secret of success is constancy to purpose.

Disraeli

Purpose is what gives life a meaning.

Charles Henry Parkhurst

ments. But if he's any good, he'll come through in the end just as you did. And there's no logical reason why you should slave in order that your daughter may have things which your own sister wasn't able to have, or in order that your wife can enjoy comforts and luxuries that she wasn't used to before she married you."

He looked at me with rather a pitying look and said, "But Mr. Gray, there's no inspiration in logic. There's no courage in logic. There's not even happiness in logic. There's only satisfaction. The only place logic has in my life is in the realization that the more I am willing to do for my wife and children, the more I shall be able to do for myself."

Imagine, after hearing that story, you won't have to be told how to find your **purpose** or how to identify it or how to surrender to it. If it's a big **purpose**, you will be big in its accomplishment. If it's an unselfish **purpose**, you will be unselfish in accomplishing it.

I believe that the intense purpose, the moral integrity, the self-loyalty that makes a man carry through whatever he undertakes is the biggest single factor in fitting his mind for great accomplishments.

Fred B. Robinson

Many persons have a wrong idea of what constitutes true happiness. It is not attained through self-gratification but through fidelity to a worthy purpose.

Helen Keller

And if it's an honest **purpose**, you will be honest and honorable in the accomplishment of it. But as long as you live, don't ever forget that while you may succeed beyond your fondest hopes and your greatest expectations, you will never succeed beyond the **purpose** to which you are willing to surrender. Furthermore, your surrender will not be complete until you have formed the habit of doing the things that failures don't like to do.

About the Author

Albert E. N. Gray first delivered his address entitled *The Common Denominator of Success* at the 1940 National Association of Life Underwriters annual convention. Business leaders, financial service and sales professionals from all arenas still continue to benefit from his relevant message that has been available in pamphlet form ever sense he first shared it.

Albert Gray was an official of the Prudential Insurance Company of America who was highly sought after nationwide as a speaker and writer of topics related to life insurance. He also had three decades of experience as a promotor, an agent in the field, and an instructor in sales development.

Since the inception of *The Common Denominator of Success* message, countless individuals have been motivated to do the things they don't like to do, in order to accomplish the things they want to accomplish.

More than any other quality, Albert Gray singled out a strong sense of purpose as one of the primary factors that motivates the successful to form the habit of doing things they don't like to do in order to accomplish the purpose they want to accomplish.

RECOMMENDED
CHARACTER BUILDING BIOGRAPHIES

Dream Big–Henrietta Mears
Mover of Men and Mountains–R.G. LeTourneau
Daily Dose Of The American Dream
Treasure In Clay– Fulton J. Sheen
A Man Who Trusted God–Daws Trotman
Amazing Faith– Bill Bright
Abandoned to God–Oswald Chambers
Philadelphia Merchant–John Wanamaker
Acres of Diamonds: The Russell Conwell Story
Great American Statesmen and Heroes
Autobiography of George Muller
Autobiography of Zig Ziglar
How Did You Do It Truett–Truett Cathy
Anointed Life–Charles Spurgeon
Jeanne Guyon: An Autobiography
Then Darkness Fled–Booker T. Washington
All Things for God–Stonewall Jackson
Carry a Big Stick–Theodore Roosevelt
Glory and Honor–Johann Sebastian Bach
Never Give In–Winston Churchill
Call of Duty–Robert E. Lee
Quiet Strength–Tony Dungy
Focus or Failure–James H. Amos, Jr.
Billionaire Secrets–Bill Bartmann
Something For Nothing–Brian Tracy
Freedom From Fear–Mark Matteson
The Fred Factor–Mark Sanborn
Ultimate Gift–Jim Stovall
Go Getter–Peter B. Kyne
Leadership Lessons– LuAn Mitchell
A Fortune to Share–Paul J. Meyer

The *Life-Changing Classics* and *Laws of Leadership* series bring you timeless wisdom in compact, affordable editions! Available now at www.TremendousLifeBooks.com!

Share the warmth, wisdom and humor of beloved speaker and author Charlie "Tremendous" Jones!

- Books
- CDs
- DVDs

...And much more at Charlie's home on the web, www.TremenodusLifeBooks.com